REMEMBER WHO YOU ARE

Robbie Venter

This book is written in honour of my mother and father
- Robert and Liezel Venter.

Copyright

All rights reserved.

No part of this book may be reproduced, distributed, or transmitted in any form or by any means, including photocopying, recording, or other electronic or mechanical methods, without the prior written permission of the author, except in the case of brief quotations embodied in critical reviews and certain other noncommercial uses permitted by copyright law

TABLE OF CONTENTS

Chapter 1: The Fall from Innocence 1

Chapter 2: The Boy Who Got Lost 13

Chapter 3: The Call to Remember - The Lion King Encounter 19

Chapter 4: The Shaper 28

Chapter 5: Access to Heaven 36

Chapter 6: The Battle Against the Religious Spirit 44

Chapter 7: The Power of Divine Identity 52

Chapter 8: Do You Accept Your Position in the Godhead?57

Chapter 10:Embracing the Divine Call to Responsibility .. 64

Chapter 11:The Throne Awaits 70

A Word of Warning

By reading this book you are crossing a threshold.

You are unlocking a truth that few dare to acknowledge, let alone pursue.

This is not a book for the fainthearted.

What lies within these pages isn't mere information, it is an initiation into something ancient, something potent that has been buried beneath centuries of distraction, waiting for those bold enough to claim it.

Before you read any further, know this: what you are about to discover has the power to change everything you think you know about yourself and your place in the world.

This is a path that, once begun, cannot be undone. If you're looking for comfort, for something that fits neatly into the life you've always known, I urge you—put this book down. Walk away. This is not for you.

But if there's a desire deep within you, insisting that there is more—more to you, more to your purpose, more to this life—then perhaps you've been called here.

These words are a gateway. But understand, crossing

through will change you. Once you open yourself to this knowledge, you will awaken a force within that cannot be subdued.

You will see your true self, a self that the world has tried to make you forget.

This journey is not safe, nor is it easy.

It requires a fierce commitment, a willingness to shed the layers of falsehood and fear.

But if you dare to enter, you will find what you have longed for— a destiny waiting to be reclaimed.

Are you ready to remember who you truly are?

Chapter 1

The Fall from Innocence

In the Beginning

In the beginning, life was beautiful. South Africa was home—it was my home. It was a place that accepted me—everything was alive, and I was a part of it. I belonged to the land, and the land belonged to me.

My younger brother and I lived free, as if the world had been made just for us. There was no fear in those days, only freedom. We were wild, unconstrained, and full of life. Every day was a new adventure, with nothing to confine us. It was pure, limitless joy.

My home felt alive and full of love. My mother and father gave us love, comfort, and security. We enjoyed connection with our family - aunts, uncles, cousins, and grandparents in those days. We were woven into something larger than ourselves; we belonged. We lived a simple life—my father a teacher, my mother a midwife. There was nothing out of the ordinary about our family.

And then, there was Rebecca. She wasn't just our maid—she was family. Her presence was powerful, and her smile was warm. She used to always play with us, providing us with that special, warm African love. There was something protective about her presence that I still remember to this day.

I had a very beautiful connection with God as a young boy, and I used to run around singing songs to Jesus. Nothing in me ever questioned His existence - it was a natural part of life.

I had a best friend who lived a few houses down from me; we used to play together almost every day, and life was perfect. It was the kind of life that felt eternal. I believed it would always be that way. Why wouldn't it? I had no reason to think otherwise.

The Day My World Changed

I'll never forget when my parents announced that we would be leaving to live in a new country. It was unheard of in our neighborhood in the 1990s for a middle-class family like mine to sell everything, leave family and jobs behind and and immigrate to a distant country. It was a major decision.

Their decision was driven by a prophecy from someone at our church that said they would leave the country.

My parents had mixed feelings about this decision, so my dad went ahead of the family, left home for a few weeks to go and check out New Zealand. It was his first time ever flying internationally. I still remember the beautiful drawing of a bird that he did for us on the window with a marker and a note for us. I missed him while he was away.

While in New Zealand, he called my mum and told her that he really wasn't sure about this decision as everything in New Zealand was so different from what they were used to at home. They both agreed to pray that night and talk again the next day. That night, they read their Bibles and both were inspired by the same scripture about Abraham leaving his mother and father's house to go on a journey of discovery with God. That was their confirmation. They agreed to make the decision, out of obedience, and said yes to the call to step into the unknown.

Looking back, this decision came at a big cost—sacrificing the known for the unknown. It was a decision that would change the trajectory of our generations. Our family line had called Africa home since the 1600s, and in a sudden decision, that reality would change.

I was eight years old at the time, and all I knew was my life in South Africa. I loved my country, loved my language, loved my school, loved my home, loved my friends. I had security, and I had safety. New Zealand was a place I couldn't even picture, a far-off land. But South Africa was everything to me. I didn't have the words to explain it, but I felt the uncertainty growing deep inside my gut.

As we were packing, it wasn't just clothes and toys being put into bags—it was my life. Every item packed away represented a part of my life disappearing. I remember saying goodbye to family and friends for the last time, saying goodbye to Rebecca, who was like a second mother, for the last time, saying goodbye to my friend Dawie and all of my extended family and my grandparents for the last time.

On the plane, I pressed my face against the window, watching Africa—my Africa—disappear beneath the clouds. It wasn't just land I was leaving behind. I was leaving behind the boy I had been—the joy I had known, the freedom that had defined me. Everything I had been was swallowed by the sky.

New Zealand

Landing in New Zealand for an eight-year-old boy

whose heart was still beating to the rhythm of Africa felt like the end of everything that was familiar to me. The moment the plane touched down, I stepped into a different world.

English was everywhere, in every sign, every voice, but it wasn't my language. My tongue stumbled over the words, twisting them into awkward shapes that made me sound like a stranger to myself. Every conversation felt like I was trapped behind a glass wall, banging my fists against it, trying to make my meaning understood, but all I got in return were confused looks. I missed the easy warmth of Afrikaans, the way my words flowed naturally. Here, every word was a struggle, and none of them felt like mine.

It wasn't just the words that were different; the kids at school had their own groups, their own jokes, their own way of being that I just couldn't seem to break into. They spoke to each other with a speed and ease that left me feeling like an outsider, always a few steps behind.

One day, I remember trying to tell a joke to a group of boys, and they all started laughing hysterically. Then one of the boys stopped and said to me, "You don't understand; we are not laughing *with* you, we are laughing *at* you." This made me feel even more unwanted in this new environment.

Some of my classmates insisted that I was a racist since I was from South Africa. Nothing could have been further from the truth, as I missed Rebecca's warm African love and her comforting energy.

My teachers didn't know what to do with a kid like me. They saw a boy who couldn't sit still, a boy who didn't pay attention to instructions, and a boy who seemed to always be in trouble. They thought I was defiant, but they didn't understand the turmoil beneath. I wasn't being difficult on purpose—I just didn't understand half of what they said. Instructions got lost in translation, and I was left floundering in a world that seemed to expect me to be someone different. Before, my energy had been something to celebrate; here, it was something to fix. They wanted me to sit quietly, to blend in, but I had far too much energy for that.

I was teased for having ginger hair, teased for being religious, and teased for being a foreigner. This was something that I had never experienced before.

I felt more and more homesick every day. I missed the songs we used to sing at our home church. I missed my grandparents' house, the smells of home-cooked meals, and the warmth of familiar stories. And I missed Rebecca, her comforting presence. I missed being known, being understood, being loved, and being accepted. There was a hole inside me where all those things had been.

Every night, I'd lie in bed and think of home, many of those nights crying myself to sleep. But no matter how hard I wished, there was no going back. My life became a series of disconnections—disconnected from my language, from my friends, from my family, and, most painfully, from myself. I felt like a tree that had been ripped from its roots, and no matter how hard I tried to settle into this new soil, it wasn't working.

I wished there was someone who could see through the confusion, who could understand the wildness that still beat in my chest—a wildness that refused to be tamed by the rigid structure of this new world.

Home

At home, the distance between my parents and me grew. They were in full-on survival mode. They moved here without jobs and had to work really hard to find work, save up a deposit, and survive. My parents were going through their own stress of immigrating and navigating a new country, with the added responsibility of building new careers and providing for the family.

As my brother and I began to adapt more to the New Zealand way of life—the slang, culture, way of dressing, music, skateboarding, etc.—we turned into people that made it more difficult for my parents to relate to. We weren't speaking the same language anymore—literally or figuratively.

In Africa, we had been connected, moving to the same rhythm, but now, that rhythm was gone. We all tried our best, and I knew they loved my brother and me more than anything in the world, but we became more and more disconnected. They didn't understand the emptiness that had settled inside me, the weight of feeling so utterly lost.

I wasn't just losing the land, I wasn't just losing myself—I was losing *them* too. Even though we lived physically in the same space, it felt like we didn't know how to understand each other like we used to.

The Drift into Rebellion

The teachers saw a problem child where there was really just a child in pain. They thought discipline would straighten me out, but every reprimand, every detention, only drove me deeper into myself, into the loneliness that was quickly becoming my constant companion. My world was shrinking, becoming smaller and colder, and no one seemed to notice that I was fading. Teachers treated me like something broken, something that needed to be fixed. From the moment I stepped into that school, it felt like I had been dropped into a machine that wasn't made for me.

The classrooms felt like prisons to me. The walls were too close, the windows too small. I felt like a caged animal, pacing, restless, suffocated. My spirit, which had once roamed free under the African sky, was now trapped, confined to this tiny, suffocating box. I wanted to run, to break free, but there was nowhere to go.

Teachers became the keepers of the cage. It didn't feel like they cared about understanding me. They cared about order, about control. I was too loud, too energetic, too inquisitive, too defiant, too much for their controlled world. Every time I acted out, I was met with punishment—detention, suspensions. Their punishments weren't just about controlling my behavior—it felt like they were trying to break my spirit by squeezing me into a mold that was never meant for me. They didn't see a boy who was lost—they saw a problem. And in their eyes, problems had to be controlled. They watched me with narrowed eyes, always expecting trouble.

No matter how hard I tried, even when I tried to behave my best, I couldn't find approval. The verdict? *There must be something wrong with him.*

My parents took me to a psychologist who ran a series of tests on me, without really taking into consideration the broader context of the situation, and quickly came to a conclusion—there is, in fact, something wrong with him. He has a deficit. And he has a disorder.

When they handed down the diagnosis—*Attention Deficit Hyperactivity Disorder*—it felt like a verdict, a label that would hang over me like a shadow. It wasn't just a medical term; it was a sentence that trapped me in a negative label.

This label has been branded on some of the brightest and bravest in society. Many powerful people in history displayed the traits that are common under this so-called disorder, including Thomas Edison, Winston Churchill, Albert Einstein, Mozart, Richard Branson, and many more brilliant people. People with this 'disorder' are out-of-the-box thinkers, innovators, creators, people who challenge the status quo. They are risk-takers, people who carve new paths for humanity to follow. But to the school system, they are a disruption. They are divergents.

Neurodivergents. And I was a carrier of this disorder.

Their solution? Ritalin—a strong drug that made me feel like a zombie. The pills dulled my edges, smoothed out the wildness, but they dulled everything else too. My joy, my spark, the part of me that felt wild—it was all sedated. They weren't just trying to control me; it felt like they were trying to tame me, erase the true me, and replace me with a compliant, more palatable version that fit within their system.

The boy who had once sung to Jesus under the African sun was fading, replaced by someone angry, someone lost.

I had tried to behave, to fit into the box they wanted me to be in. But their world wasn't made for someone like me. So, I decided, if I couldn't fit in, I would break out. Every boundary I pushed, every rule I broke—it was all a desperate attempt to reclaim some sense of control. I would not yield to the system designed to capture and erase me.

One day, in a final act of defiance, I was seen by a teacher skipping class again. When he finally caught up with me, I decided that I was done. I pulled out a cigarette in front of my teacher, it was time to put an end to this, I lit it up right in front of him in a final act of defiance. I was expelled and asked never to return.

The Breaking Point

After I was expelled, my life became a series of failures. I drifted from job to job, never able to hold on to anything. The boy who had once been full of life and joy was gone, replaced by a shell of a person who no longer cared about anything. My life spiraled further out of control. I had no money. No direction. No future. Thousands of dollars in fines. Alcohol had become my escape. It felt like I had nothing left.

The breaking point for me came on my eighteenth birthday. Some guy who I had insulted years ago wanted to fight me. A bunch of my friends gathered around me to protect me from him, but when the police arrived on the scene, they arrested me. They forced me into the back of the police truck with all their strength as I resisted. It was a cold winter's night in July. The police took my warm top off me, saying that there was a risk that I could use it to try and hang myself. I spent the whole night freezing cold without any sleep in the cells with other criminals. Had I become a criminal? I had become everything they said I was—a failure, a problem, a boy with a deficit and a disorder.

Chapter 2

The Boy Who Got Lost

The Grief of Losing Yourself

There is a different kind of grief you experience when you realize you've lost yourself. It's not like losing your keys, losing a job, or losing a relationship. It's a primal grief—deep, raw, and searing. You wake up one morning and see someone staring back at you that you don't recognize. Your gut tells you that you are living a lie, that the person you see in the mirror isn't the true version of you. Others may not see through the masks, but you know they're there.

That grief hit me when I thought back about who I used to be. Memories found their way to the surface, pulling me back to a time when life was untouched by pain. I remembered playing on the swing my dad made for my brother and me in our backyard in South Africa. The memory of that little Robbie haunted me—the boy who laughed, the boy who was free, the boy who was *alive*. And more than anything, the boy who was friends with God.

But looking back at him now, it felt like I was watching someone else's life—a life that wasn't mine. That boy—the one who felt the presence of God, was gone. And in his place stood a man who had drowned himself in addictions, so far lost he couldn't see a way back. *Where did he go? Where had I gone?*

I was grieving the loss of myself.

The Breakdown

As I thought about my life—the arrest, the fines, the jobs I kept losing, the school I was expelled from, and my absolute inability to imagine where I was going—I realized that I couldn't handle it anymore. Life was unbearable. It all came crashing down. The masks, the lies, the anger—it all crumbled. I couldn't pretend anymore.

Was it time to end it all? Suicidal thoughts circled my mind like vultures, hungry for my soul.

I had some amazing friends, who were there for me, who I loved dearly, but they couldn't understand what I was going through, and they couldn't help me.

Something inside of me caved in. I wasn't the tough guy

anymore. I wasn't the one in control. I was a wreck.

I cried out to God—not in some nice prayer, but in a raw, desperate scream for help. I had hit rock bottom. I couldn't see any way out. *If God didn't step in, I was done.*

The Vision

Not long after that desperate cry, I had a vision that would alter the course of my life.

I saw myself hanging on the edge of a cliff, clinging to a patch of grass, knowing that if it snapped, I would fall to my death. My heart pounded with fear, every muscle straining to hold on.

And then, *I saw Him.*

Jesus stood there with 100% focus on me. Standing on the edge of the cliff, His hand outstretched toward me. His eyes weren't full of judgment—they radiated compassion and strength. He wasn't angry. He wasn't disappointed. He was *present*.

"Take My hand," He said. "Before it's too late."

Something in me—something buried deep, buried under all the pain and anger—reached out. I grabbed His hand. It was instinct. It was survival. *I didn't want to die.*

In that moment, something in my life shifted.

The Miracle Call

During this time, my parents were so worried about me, but I didn't know that they were praying and fasting for me. Yet, I could feel things moving—shifts I couldn't explain. God was at work. Looking back, I realize that if they hadn't been praying for me, my life could very well have been lost.

A few days later, the phone rang. My father's voice was on the other end, carrying news that felt like a miracle. My aunt in South Africa, who I hadn't spoken to in years, had reached out. She told him that God had put me on her heart. She didn't know exactly what I was going through, didn't know how far I had fallen, but she *knew.* She knew I needed help. Heaven's informants had reached her after I had taken the hand of Jesus.

She offered me a lifeline—a chance to come live with her in South Africa for a year. It was a door I hadn't even known existed, it felt too perfect to be a coincidence. This was divine intervention. It had to be.

Now, I had a choice. Stay where I was, drowning in the

darkness, or take the chance, pack up everything I had, and leave. Leave the shadows behind.

The Spiritual Battle on the Plane

Waving goodbye to my friends and family at the airport stirred a familiar ache of leaving my life behind, but this time I was leaving New Zealand to return to Africa. I loved my friends and saying goodbye to them was not an easy choice. Ten years earlier, I had flown in the opposite direction, filled with uncertainty. Now, I was retracing my steps.

The plane ride back to South Africa was more than just a physical journey—it was a spiritual battle. As I sat in that seat, memories flooded me, voices from the past intensified—every mistake, every failure, every moment of regret. The enemy wasn't done with me yet. He whispered in my ear, *You're not worth anything, nobody wants you. You can't change. You're not worth saving.*

It was a war raging in my mind, a tug of war over my destiny. The armies of heaven and the armies of hell clashed, and I could feel the weight of their struggle. It was as if all the events of the last ten years had been leading up to this moment, a moment where every decision I had made was being challenged and weighed.

Touching Down in South Africa

When the plane touched down, it wasn't just a return to a place—it was a return to my destiny. I stepped off the plane, and the African sun hit me, wrapping me in its warmth. The smells, the languages, the familiar embrace of family—it all rushed back, flooding my senses with memories I had long buried. Seeing my grandmother and my aunty was one of the best moments for me, to be greeted by them at the airport triggered so many memories that I thought were lost.

For the first time in a long time, I felt the stirrings of the boy I used to be. That boy who sang to Jesus, who trusted that life could be good, who believed in miracles. I knew the journey had just begun, but in that moment, I also knew that God was with me.

The path ahead was uncertain, but this time, I wasn't walking it alone.

Chapter 3

The Call to Remember - The Lion King Encounter

Returning to South Africa felt nostalgic. It felt like the ten years since I had left had passed quickly. Not much had changed in South Africa, but I had changed. It felt like a part of me was being reawakened. One night, I found myself in a packed theater, waiting for *The Lion King* to begin. I didn't know that I had been set up - that this was a divine appointment. A few weeks earlier I cried out to God, now I was on the other side of the world watching a show in Johannesburg.

With the lights dimming, I closed my eyes and whispered, "God, You promised to leave the ninety-nine to find the one. I am lost come and find me." My heart was desperate for direction, for guidance, for answers. The forces fighting over my destiny felt very real. I was in a very vulnerable state.

The first notes of *The Circle of Life* played through the massive speakers. The stage flickered to life. The savannah appeared, and I was being pulled into a story that would change my life.

The Theater of Souls

As Simba came onto the stage, I felt a deep connection with him. He was the heir, chosen to be the next King. He carried an important destiny. He was untouched by pain, connected to his family, connected to his home, connected to his destiny and connected to his father, connected to his own heart. Watching the show, I thought back to that version of me that once held that same fire, that same innocence.

But as you know if you've watched the Lion King, that phase of his life didn't last long. His evil uncle Scar was lurking on the sidelines, a predator who craved the throne that Simba was destined to have.

Scars evil plan to claim the throne for himself started by him subtly planting seeds of deception in Simbas mind. Planning to take what was his and steal his destiny. Then, Simbas world came crashing down. Scar killed Mufassa. In Simbas moment of deepest pain, Scar took advantage of the situation by deceving Simba, filling his mind with guilt, fear and shame.

"Run, Simba, run. And never return," he hissed, with a demonic ring to his voice.

Simba lost everything that was dear to him, his home, his family, his sense of identity. In a moment of vulnerability he allowed the voice of the enemy to penetrate his heart. Scar convinced him that he was unworthy, unwanted and should never return to the place of his throne. An evil plot to take the throne for himself. As I was watching this I recognized the tactic—the same ancient deception thats been used against us for thousands of years. A lie that tells us we are disqualified, unworthy, that we dont belong and that we should run away from our destiny.

I realised that the voices I heard on the plane over to South Africa were not my own thoughts, they were the voice of an enemy who wanted me to give up hope and run from my destiny.

The *Hakuna Matata* Illusion

As Simba fled, he stumbled into a world of "no worries"—a place where he could drown his past in distractions. *Hakuna Matata* became his motto, a lifestyle offering an illusion of peace. But beneath it all, Simba knew that he was living a lie. He knew that he was destined for greatness. He burried the voice of his father, forgot who he was and lived a life that he pretended that he was happy with. He thought that it was no longer possible to be the king he was called to be, he thought he was unfit, unworthy, and unwanted.

Watching Simba settle into this life of ease, I saw a reflection of myself, and of countless others who've chosen comfort over calling, who've buried their identity under layers of distraction. All these years, I've tried to bury the voice of the Spirit trying to remind me that I was destined for something greater.

Even in this phase of his life, Simbas destiny was still present. We cant run from our destiny for long, even when we try to escape. As Simba grew, the King inside of him didn't die; it only went dormant, waiting for the day that he'd remember. As Simba ignored his destiny, the kingdom that he was called to rule lay in ruins under Scar's evil reign, crying for its true king. Every day Simba stayed in hiding, his kingdom went deeper into darkness. The absence of the King, made the land suffer.

The Divine Messenger and the Mirror

Then, Rafiki appeared, the wise monkey messenger - he came to reconect Simba with his father. With a knowing smile, he said "Come with me." His voice resounding with ancient African knowledge. He came to confront Simba. To confront his denial of who he was and what he was called to.

Rafiki led Simba to a quiet pool—a mirror, a place of revelation. As Simba gazed into the water, he saw only a broken reflection, the shell of who he once was. Rafiki whispered: "Look harder. See - He lives in you".

The Voice of the Father

A storm gathered, with the sound of thunder as the heavens opened, and from the swirling clouds, Simba's father, Mufasa appeared. He embodied a deep love and authority. AS he spoke in a deep and powerful voice, the entire theater disolved and I was drawn into an encounter with my Father.

Mufasa's voice was piercing. "Simba," he called,

- "you have forgotten me"
- "you have forgotten who you are."
- And so you've forgoten me

- Look inside yourself
- You are more than what you have become
- You must take your place

In that moment, something broke open within me. Elecrticity surging through my body, this was a supernatural encounter.

Those words weren't just for Simba; they were for me. "You are more than what you have become," Mufasa continued.

- SImba responded
- How can I go back? Im not who I used to be.
- Remember who you are.
- You are my son
- The one true king
- Remember who you are
- Remember.

Tears flowed through my eyes. The parts of my heart that were shut down for years opened up. The God of the universe used this moment to speak directly to me. The power and love that I felt from the spirit of God at that moment was incredible. Years of lies, years of pain, years of deception falling off me in that moment of time.

Reclaiming What is Yours

Simba stood there wrestling with what just happened. Is it real? Is it true? Am I still the appointed king? But so much time has passed? Do I have what it takes? I have been living a lie for so long.

Two voices fighting over his destiny the voice inside of him that came into agreement with the enemy and the voice of his father.

It all came down to a decision. A decision to come into agreement with his father. Agreeing with the truth is not always easy. Reclaiming your identity is not a passive process but a fierce struggle against both internal and external forces.

Simba returned to confront the very force that had stolen his inheritance, robbed him of his identity, and taken his throne. He stopped bowing to the lie that whispered "run away and never return" he was ready to reclaim his place.

Watching that battle, I felt the intensity of my own internal war. I thought about the suicidal voices, the lies, the deceiver who had tried to kill me. Scar was a symbol of every dark force that longs to see us destroyed.

The final battle was epic. Simba had to confront his enemy and evict him from the place that he was illegaly occupying. Demonic entities want your throne just like Scar wanted Simbas throne. Scar put up a fight but he didnt prevail, Simba tapped into a primal and eternal strength. The strength that allows good to overcome evil. After an epic battle, Simba secured the victory.

As Simba took back the throne, the land blossomed once more. Rivers flowed, life returned, and the kingdom was restored. I realized then that this journey wasn't just about personal victory—it was about a great restoration that reached far beyond myself, a ripple effect that would have an impact far beyond me. That as sons and daughters take their place, the prayer of Christ would be answered and it would be on earth as it is in heaven. There is a direct correlation between us occupying our designated place of rulership and the great restoration that will unfold in creation.

The Choice to Remember

As the final chords of the performance played, I sat there feeling like I was tane outside of time, lived many years and was put back into time. In earth time the show was only a couple of hours long but in the Spirit I had experienced what felt like a lifetime of revelation unlocked in a single moment.

God had spoken through this story, calling me back to the truth of who I was. I walked out of that theater with Mufasa's words echoing in my heart: "Remember who you are." For the first time in years, I was starting to remember. I chose to defeat every force that tried to make me forget, every lie that tried to keep me small.

But the choice isn't just for me—it's for you, too. You, are being called to your own awakening, you are called to rise, to reclaim what has always been yours.

Chapter 4
The Shaper

Awakening from a Deep Sleep

After *The Lion King*, a part of me—buried under years of lies, labels and judgments—was coming alive, awakening to a call I'd almost forgotten. But shaking off the a false version of yourself you've unknowingly built, isn't instant. It's a journey. I had internalized the labels. Years of being the black sheep, being labeled as "troubled," the boy with the "disorder," the one who never quite fit in.

It was time to come into agreement with the right voice and become the real Robbie. Just like Simba went through a phase of accepting, it was my turn to internalise a new identity. An identity based on truth.

Meeting Des: The Untamed Spirit

Not long after that night in the theater, I heard about a gap-year program called Surfmasters. I can still remember the moment I found out about it. I knew I had to go. It was my next step in this divinely orchestrated path. My application was sent in, I wasnt exactly the model candidate for a bible shcool. With a history of like mine, I seriously doubted that they would accept me.

It wasnt long after the application was sent that I was accepted. I made the trip to Jeffreys Bay, South Africa and met Des and Cara for the first time. Des and Cara opened their home to 12 other young people from many countries around the world. Dedicating their lives and sacrificing their time to facilitate true discipleship. A form of discipleship that cost them a lot. Cara carried an aura of love and filled the environment with her love. Des was challenging, confrontational and unpredictable.

I also met a young woman at Surfmasters called Jazz, when I met her I knew she was special. She was beautiful, exotic, wild. Her eyes sparkling with a curiosity that was both playful and intense. She definitely caught my attention, but I will tell you more about Jazz later in the book.

Des was a man you couldn't pin down. His spirit was untamed, his views unfiltered, and he seemed to move through life with the confidence of someone who had been broken and rebuilt with nothing to fear. Des reminded me of Rafiki from *The Lion King*, a wise, untamed prophet who saw through the noise and straight into the heart of things. He didn't tiptoe around truth to make you feel good; he cared more about your destiny than your comfort. He saw through the masks I wore—the masks everyone else seemed to accept as "Robbie"—and believed in me in a way no one ever had. He would push me, challenge me, and ultimately help me remember who I truly was.

A Channel for the Spirit

Des's voice wasn't just a voice; it was a spiritual *force*. He spoke with the kind of power that came not from human intellect, but from something beyond, something eternal. Every morning we would gather on the Surfmasters deck, ready to hear what Des had to say. Des came down the stairs he transformed into a conduit for revelation, a man full of the Spirit. Nothing he said was rehearsed or polished. It was raw, powerful and real.

The deck itself felt sacred, it was our temple, it felt like stepping into the cave of an ancient prophet. Wooden beams weathered by salt and sea framed our gathering place. Des's eyes seemed to glimmer, as if they held a thousand secrets, just waiting to be spoken. For some, this intensity was too much to handle. But for me? I couldn't get enough. It was as if I was witnessing a kind of spiritual mastery, a level of presence that is rare.

Each lesson dismantling more of the lies and layers that had built up over years. Des had this uncanny way of speaking directly to the parts of me that needed to be adressed. He would look at you, and it felt like he could see straight through you. His words were precise, cutting through with an insight that left me both shaken and renewed. He seemed to know things about my life, my struggles, even my future—like he could see the trajectory of my journey long before I could.

He was everything my former teachers weren't. While they'd labeled me, dismissed me, made me feel like I was a problem, Des saw past the labels, straight to the truth of who I was. He didn't see someone broken; he saw potential, fire, purpose. He saw a world changer. Being seen, understood, loved and accepted was the greatest gift anyone could have ever given me. For Des, teaching was an art of *extraction*, not *insertion*. He didn't try to impose beliefs on us; instead, he unlocked what was already inside. With each word, he was pulling out gifts and callings, hidden strengths and forgotten dreams. It was as if the Spirit guided him to see each person's potential with a clarity that left me in awe. Watching Des in action was witnessing what it meant to be fully alive, fully led by the Spirit, fully committed to a purpose that transcended self.

He didn't lean on old sermons or recite principles out of habit. No, he was filled with the Spirit in a way that made every word he spoke resonate on a level I can hardly describe. It felt as if he wasn't the one speaking but that he'd opened himself up to be a channel, allowing the Spirit to pour through him. For someone like me, someone who had spent years feeling unseen, to witness this kind of pure spiritual power was a gift straight from God Himself.

Des's voice wasn't just a voice; it was an invitation. It's time to rise." And he didn't just say it; he *believed* it for me when I couldn't believe it for myself. His confidence in my destiny made me believe that I was worthy, capable, and ready to claim the life that had always been waiting for me.

Shaping the Surfboard, Shaping the Soul

One day, Des invited me into his shaping bay—a space filled with the scent of resin and sawdust, boards in various stages of completion leaning against the walls. With a rough hand, he ran his fingers over a half-finished board, looking at it with reverence. "You know what shaping is really about?" he asked, his voice low, charged with mystery. "It's not about adding. It's about stripping away everything that isn't needed."

Shaping wasn't about creating something; it was about revealing what was already there. Des learned through years of shaping to be able to see an individuals shape. Meaning who God created them to be. And his job was to cut away everything that doesnt matach the trtuth of who that person is. This is what Des was doing for me, what he was drawing out with every lesson, every look, every challenge. The labels, the lies, the scars—they were being stripped away, like layers being stripped from the board until only the truest part of me remained.

I got an insight into the hidden place where God taught Des for years how to disciple people.

The Weeds That Choked Me

One day, as I walked alone down the road, my eyes fell on a plant growing beside the road. At first, it looked healthy but as I got closer, I noticed a weed had wrapped around the plant so tightly it was hard to distinguish the weed from the plant. I stopped and bent down an looked closely at how this invasive weed had twisted itself around the plant. And in that moment, God's voice came to me, clear as day: "There are things in your life that you think are part of who you are, but they are not. They're choking you, and I am going to remove them."

The beliefs I had carried, the labels that had shaped me—they were not mine. They were weeds, wrapped so tightly around my identity that I had mistaken them as being a part of me. That was the moment I understood what was happening. Just as Des stripped away the layers from his surfboards, God was stripping away every lie and false belief that had wrapped itself around my soul.

The Power of Surrender

From that day on, I committed myself to the process of surrender, to the shedding of every layer that didn't align with the truth of who I was. It wasn't an easy road. It felt like tearing away pieces of myself. But with each act of surrender, I felt lighter. I was no longer carrying the weight of who I thought I should be—I was becoming who I was always meant to be.

The Becoming

Des found me broken on the roadside, he lifted me up, spoke truth into my life, and reminded me of my value. The year at Surfmasters was another divine appointment along this path that God was taking me on. But now, it was time to go back and deal with some unfinished business back in New Zealand.

Chapter 5
Access to Heaven

A Return to New Zealand

Leaving South Africa was like stepping out of a dream. As the plane descended over New Zealand, I looked down at the familiar landscape, and realized just how much I had changed. My parents were there at the airport, beaming with a joy that only comes when prayers are finally answered. I could see it in their eyes. I knew I was stepping into a new chapter, and they were right there with me.

Back home, things were different. My parents and I grew closer together. My mothers prayers paid off and the pain and misunderstandings of the past were being replaced by a relationship of love and connection. My parents went out of their way to welcome me home and honoured the transformation they saw in my life. My father started helping me shape my future. He took me to investing conferences, introduced me to inspirational people, challenged me to read books and opened the door to an opportunity to work for a local real estate company.

Not long after I started at the real estate company, I met Barry Ward, the best real estate agent in town, a man with a reputation for taking great care of his clients. Barry took me in as a a nineteen-year-old in an industry that didnt have room for kids that age. He treated me with respect, asked for my input, trusted me with important tasks and valued me as an equal. He treated me as an equal business partner. Through him, I saw something of the Father's heart—patient, loving, but dedicated to his purpose. He gave me not just mentorship but the confidence that would lay the foundation for the life I'd build and my future prosperity.

During this time New Zealand transformed into a place of blessing, favour, growth and abundance. I didnt know that the inspiration from my father and Barry's support, would create the foundation for me to create an incredible investment portfolio.

By remembering, remembering who I was, it felt like the world was responding differently to me. God was showing me different aspects of his nature through different people that he was placing on my path. He was introducing me to

His friends. My aunty's phone call, the lion king concert, Des and Cara Sawyer, my Mums prayers, my Fathers support, Barry's kindness and this was just the beginning. When we accept God, we also accept those who are connected to Him and He finds ways to introduce us to His friends.

As I continued down my path, I was grateful for all that was unfolding in my life, but there was still a longing I couldn't quite name. I knew there was more. I knew it. I just didn't know where to look. When we pray and ask God for more, its a dangerous prayer and isnt always answered on our terms.

A Mysterious Encounter at the Pools

One quiet afternoon, I made my way to the local hot pools in Napier for a swim. As I arrived at the pools, the air was filled with steam, the ocean waves breaking in the background. Across the pools, I noticed a man sitting alone in a hot tub. He looked familiar, though I couldn't place him at first. Then I realized—I'd seen him at my parents' church years ago. I felt a pull, a gravity to him, almost magnetic. I felt that I needed to speak to him, but I didnt know why.

I went and sat next to him and introduced myself. There was an intensity in his eyes that caught me off guard, similar to Des when he was preaching to us on the Surfmasters deck. This man was seeing past the surface, past everything. He had the kind of presence that made the air feel charged.

"Ian Clayton," he said, introducing himself.

I felt that same sense that this was a divine appointment, a divine introduction. Ian wasn't here to chat about the weather. There was a purpose in his gaze, a clarity that was almost otherworldly. He seemed to know something that I was looking for but didn't yet know.

"You know," he began, "you don't have to wait for Heaven."

His words were confronting. I had been taught that Heaven is something distant, something promised as a reward for later, something we enter after death, something unattainable in this life. I had grown up believing Heaven was for the afterlife. It was the final destination.

His statement didn't fit anywhere in my framework.

"What do you mean?" I asked feeling curious, frustrated and excited at the same time.

Ian spoke again, with a determined look in his eyes. "Heaven isn't a place you reach after you die," he said.

"Heaven is as close as the air you breathe. Its not about distance, its about dimension. You can choose to turn into it and live from it"

It felt like my mind was a blackboard and Ian was wiping everything away. These words were going against the grain of my existing understanding. He was revealing a dimension that had always been there, waiting to be noticed. Heaven was here? Heaven was *now*?

"How... how is that possible?" I managed to ask, grappling with what he was saying.

With the same intensity, he started sharing more

"You are a spirit being. Not a human being"

Ian was explaining that as Spirit beings we have the ability to function in the Spiritual world of our Father - heaven. Its a dimension that we have full access to. His sense of frustration and impatience came from the fact that very few believers are aware of this truth, let alone function in this reality.

"Jesus tore the veil," he said. "You have full, unhindered access to Heaven now. But you have to choose to turn into it."

My mind was racing confused by these concepts, but something else in me was wide awake, recognizing truth in his words. If anyone else had said these things to me, I'd be very tempted to dismiss them. But there was something about the man in front of me, that felt like he had walked in the reality that he was describing. There was a depth in his words, a resonance in his voice that was different. He spoke with authority, an authority that came from another world.

Staring into his eyes, as he spoke, it was like time stood still. I was weighing him up. Is he telling the truth or is he lying and making all of this up? I can spot a liar pretty easily and it didnt feel like Ian was lying. But what he was talking about seemed so out there, I had never even heard of this perspective before.

As Ian spoke, I felt the pull of his invitation. I had seen the miraculous nature of Gods hand on my life. I had taken the hand of Jesus in that vision, I had seen how making a choice in a vision could have a powerful impact on our lives, but Ian's understanding on the realm of heaven was beyond anything I had ever seen before.

I was curious, I was intrigued, but there was also fear—fear of the unknown, of stepping into a reality that I couldnt figure out or control. This wasn't just a small shift in perspective, this was a whole new way of viewing reality.

The Fork in the Road

I had no idea who I was talking to on that day. No idea that Ian was a pioneer in the faith that he travels speaking at conferences, that he has inspired people all over the world and reshaped peoples perspectives on heaven. That was no doubt another divine appointment, a pivital moment for me.

Ians words carried the weight of a challenge, a choice. I could sense that he was offering me a path, but this was no ordinary path. It was a path that could change everything, one that demanded that I give up believing I had everything figured out. Part of me wanted to run, to cling to the safety of what I knew. Another part of me wanted to experience the realms he was talking about.

When we finally parted ways, Ian's words stayed with me. This was no ordinary conversation. This was a door opening, a glimpse into a reality that was both terrifying and beautiful. This was an invitation to a new way of *being*. An invitation to access another dimension. But stepping through that door was a choice that I hadn't made yet. Heaven was within reach, but the decision to live from it wouldn't be an easy choice.

Would I step in? Or would I retreat into the familiar

Chapter 6

The Battle Against the Religious Spirit

Standing at Heaven's Door

I felt like I was standing on the edge of something ancient, a realm that deep down, I knew existed but had forgotten how to access. I could feel the pulse of heaven. I could feel the potential of heaven, I could feel the invitation of heaven.

His words kept swirling in my mind : *"Heaven is as close to you as the air that you breathe"* The door was open, the price had been paid for my access, the veil was torn, the invitation was there.

But in between me and the door stood two big obstacles. Most people neverovercomethese obstacles and unfortunately miss out on so much of what God has made available.

Obstacle Number 1 - Logic

The first obstacle was my own logic. We forget that we are spirit beings, we have a soul and a body, but there is a part of us that the **permanent** and **primary** part of who we are - the eternal part of who we are. **Spirit**. As Ian would remind me, you don't have a spirit you are a Spirit and you have a body. But for most of us we have forgotten how to function out of the primary part of who we truly are. For the first time, I began to understand: I wasn't just a body. I was spirit, made for eternity, with an open invitation to my Father's world.

I'd been passing over scriptures for years, skimming over their meaning, blind to the invitation in them. *Come boldly to the throne,* they said. *We are seated with Christ in heavenly places.* They were truths I'd been sleeping through, truths that had become so familiar that I'd missed their power. Scripture encourages us to worship in the spirit, walk in the spirit, be lead by the spirit. It affirms that God is Spirit, and we are made in his image. But for many of us, even if we accept this as true, we haven't yet experienced this truth, because at some level we don't really believe it or we think it is for later. We are one with God now - whoever is joined to the Lord is one Spirit with him. The eternal part of who you are is already fully intertwined with Him and dying one day will not bring you any closer to him than you already are.

My logic was saying how can I be in heaven and on the earth at the same time? My mind was struggling to accept that I was a multi dimensional being with the capacity to function in both realms at once. How can I be a citizen of heaven? How can I be seated in Christ in heavenly places? How can I boldly approach the throne? How can I step through the veil? How can I access this dimension that Ian is talking about. How, how, how. I was trying to figure it out.

I chose to accept the truth even though to my own mind it made no sense. And as I began to meditate on the truth of scripture, not just taking Ians word for it, but thoroughly researching for myself what the word actually says, I realised that this perspective is completely biblical. We have been transferred into the Kingdom of his son. It doesn't say we will be transferred but we have been transferred (past tense).

As I meditated on these truths, as I accepted the invitation to enter for myself, as I allowed my mind to be transformed by the truth described in scripture, I began to have an attitude of faith instead of skepticism. I began to be open, hungry and excited about experiencing the reality of my Fathers world in this life. I stopped looking to death as the doorway to heaven and recognized Christ as the doorway to heaven. I realised that we have been born again from above, meaning we have been reborn into a higher dimension. We are in this world but not of this world, so we are from another world and we have full access to the world that we are from - Our Fathers world.

For me this process was much like tuning the frequency knob of a radio. Right now there are many different radio waves flowing through the air, but the frequency you turn the radio to will determine the sound that you hear and the music that plays. I began to shift my mind to come into agreement with the truth, to shift my own receptors to tune into the reality of heaven. It required a shift in my own mind to break out of limited thinking and tune into this reality.

Obstacle Number 2 - The Religious Spirit

Just as I felt ready to move, to leave the comfortable and familiar behind, something held me back. I could feel a voice, subtle at first, but present. *This is dangerous. Don't overstep your place. Heaven isn't for now.* These words came in direct opposition to the invitation from heaven. It pretended to protect me from harm, but underneath, I could tell it was scared that I would enter into a dimension it had no access to. It reminded me of Scar telling Simba that he has no place in his Kingdom.

The religious spirit typically doesn't yell. It whispers—quiet lies that can feel like truth. It doesn't deny Heaven outright; it simply places it just out of reach, saying, *"Heaven is real, but it's not for now. Be humble. Don't go too far. Stay safe."* There it was again, that twisted voice of restraint. But every inch of me could feel it: this was a trap, a trap to keep me outside.

A tug-of-war began, a tension between two forces: the voice of Jesus, saying, *"Come, I have torn the veil."* And the other voice saying, *"Turn back. Do not enter."* I knew the stakes. The religious spirit understood that if I crossed this threshold, its grip on me would break. It would lose its power. It wasn't trying to protect me; it was trying to *control* me.

The Battle for My Inheritance

This struggle wasn't new. It was the same ancient battle that had started centuries ago. Before Satan was cast out of Heaven, he wanted two things that weren't his to have.

First, he craved *identity*—he said, *"I will be like the Most High."*

Second, he wanted *position*—*"I will exalt my throne above the stars of God."*

But neither belonged to him. He wanted a Godlike form, capacity, identity, but he was not a Godlike species - he was an angel. He wanted a governmental position that wasn't his to occupy.

Then came the war. Michael and his angels fought and the devil and his angels were defeated. Satan lost it all—position, power, access, and honor. He was cast out. Imagine the bitterness of that loss. Stripped of power, Satan licked his wounds, plotting revenge.

And then God did the unthinkable. He made us in His image and likeness (the very thing that Satan wanted) and then He placed *us*—in the same arena.

And in Revelations we read *"To him who overcomes, I will grant that they sit with me on my throne."* WE are promised a governmental position within the house of God, which is what Satand craved and was denied.

Raging with hatred, he could no longer try and defeat God, but looking at us he saw the exact resemblance of the one who denied, his request, stripped him of his power, revoked his heavenly citizenship and cast him out.

So we carry the very things he wants more than anything but can never have

1. We are made in God's image, he is not.
2. We are offered a position of authority in God's kingdom, he is denied.
3. We are citizens of heaven - he lost his citizenship.

This is why he never wants you to step through the veil. Because the moment you do, you begin to operate in the truth of who you are, where you've been positioned and access all that is available to you as a son or daughter of God. Thats why there is such fierce resistance around walking in these things.

If you begin to step through the veil, believe me you will be misunderstood. You will face opposition. You will face resistance. People will turn against you. You will trigger Satan's rage. But, there is nothing he can do about it, unless you allow the voice of that spirit to block you.

Breaking Free from the Chains

This was the moment. I felt it down to my core: if I didn't step forward now, if I didn't leave the lies behind, I'd always be held back. I had to choose. I could stay in the shadows of the familiar, the predictable, or I could step into the fullness of Heaven's reality.

The religious spirit grew desperate, whispering louder,

clawing at me, *"This is reckless. Don't go. You'll lose yourself."* But I knew the truth now. I wasn't an intruder or a guest. I was a son.

I finally made the decision. I broke all agreement with this spirit. I stepped forward, shaking off the lies. I crossed that threshold, the choice final. There was no turning back. I had made the decision to enter.

I want to take a moment to honour Ian for his contribution to my life. Ian and I became great friends and he has been an incredible mentor to me over the years. Many people are skeptical of him and what he talks about, but I have watched him behind the scenes for more than a decade and can vouch for his genuine love, integrity, pursuit of the Father and relentless service to the body of Christ.

Chapter 7
The Power of Divine Identity

Experiencing Heaven

As I overcame the religious spirit and opened my heart to the truth of my access to heaven, I began to experience heaven for myself. I could feel that Heaven was drawing me in to see myself as I truly was. I began to see from a different perspective,

The Moment of Encounter

One day, as I tuned my heart into heaven, these Radiant figures surrounded me, their presence so intense. Their gaze was intense and I had never felt that level of attention on me. It made me feel seen in a way that I had never felt seen before. And I cant say that it felt comfortable. It felt safe, but exposing at the same time. WE cant hide who we are in heaven. In heaven everyone can see through your masks. And then, one of them spoke, his voice both strong and tender, ringing with an undeniable truth: *"Look at him. He looks just like his Father."*

The words shocked me. They weren't just speaking *to* me; they were proclaiming something *over* me. I felt the weight of those words settle into every part of me. Are they talking about me? He looks just like his Father? They saw my true self—a son who bore his Father's likeness. Heaven saw it. God saw it. And now, I was being invited to see it, too.

Realizing I Was the Same Kind

The implications of what I was seeing began to shock me. I had always know on one level that I was a child of God, but I realised that I had no idea what that meant until I had this encounter. According to 1 John 3:9 we are born of God and His seed is in us. That word seed is the Greek word Sperma which is where we get the word sperm from. We are reborn from His DNA - His genetic pattern. Through this encounter I saw a truth that I wouldn't have understood otherwise - I am the offspring of God in a very literal sense. He has passed his DNA onto me. Thats why they said, look at him, he looks just like his Father.

I realised for the first time that the born again part of me, the Spirit part of me, the eternal part of me and the true part of me, is the same species as God. His divine DNA was in me, I was born of Him, carrying His own nature within me. My mind was spinning with this truth as I allowed it to transform me. Stepping through the veil opened my eyes for the first time to begin to accept the reality of who I really am.

The Wrestle with Identity

But accepting this truth was no simple task. It felt like a wrestling match between the revelation I'd been given and the beliefs I'd been holding onto for so long. A part of me was asking if this was real. Familiar voices crept in, whispering that I wasn't worthy, that I was just pretending. *"Who do you think you are?" "You'll never measure up."*

I could feel the tension, the tug of war between what Heaven had shown me and what I had always believed. This wasn't just about a nice experience; it was about dismantling years of false identity, years of self-doubt. My heart wanted to believe, to step into the fullness, but the old beliefs were fighting back.

A Deeper Call: You Are More Than What You

HaveBecome

In the struggle, God kept revealing mindsets I had accepted that were out of alignment with the truth, reminding me of that powerful moment in *The Lion King* when Mufasa tells Simba, "You are more than what you have become." It wasn't just an invitation to remember; it was a call to rise above the limits I'd accepted.

God was confronting me. It was time to shed every limited perspective that I carried around my own identity. Heaven was challenging me to remember who I was—to reconnect with a truth I'd either forgotten or never fully understood. Could I accept this? Would I dare to see myself as Heaven saw me, or would I cling to the safer sense of inadequacy? It was far easier for me to see myself as a small, humble servant, a sinner, someone small who had no real value than it was to see the truth of who I was as a son and an heir carrying divine DNA.

"It's time you see yourself the way I see you."

"Its time that you esteem yourself the way that I esteem you".

God was helping me to shift my own estimation of my value. The value I placed on myself didnt align with the value

He placed on me.

Jesus is fully God, and He valued us so deeply that He exchanged His life for ours. In doing so, He set the measure of our value at the highest possible price: God's own life. By offering His life, He made a powerful statement that our lives are worth the life of God Himself.

To accept my identity as His offspring meant letting go of every sense of inadequacy, of every lesser view of myself I had ever held. Heaven had shown me who I was, but the choice to remember, to embrace, rested with me. To embrace this truth isn't easy. It's uncomfortable. It requires breaking ties with every belief that's kept you limited. But Heaven is waiting for you to remember who you are, to step into the fullness of your identity.

Chapter 8

Do You Accept Your Position in the Godhead?

Revelations

To him who overcomes I will grant to sit with Me on My throne, as I also overcame and sat down with My Father on His throne.

A Vision of Divine Positioning

One night, as I was spending time with God stepping through the veil, everything around me seemed to fade, and I was drawn into a realm that felt more real, more solid, than this physical plane. Before me stood an ancient throne, unmoved by time, powerful beyond description. It was positioned on the top of a high mountain and it was in the shadows. Beneath it lay a frozen river, silent and still. But even in this stillness, the throne radiated an authority that seemed strangely familiar to me. It was as if it had been waiting, waiting for this moment for a very long time.

Then I felt God's presence beside me - filling the atmosphere. His voice spoke in a quiet but firm tone, weighted with the kind of authority that leaves no room for doubt. He gestured toward the throne, and said *"Sit."*

I froze. Resistance rose up in me, the instinctive fear of standing before something that felt too holy, too profound. Every instinct in me screamed that this was too much. How could I, a flawed human, sit in a place I had only ever envisioned as God's alone? My mind pushing back with beliefs that had defined me as a servant, not a ruler; a follower, not one with authority. The thought of kneeling felt safe, familiar. But here, in this moment, God was asking me to do the unthinkable: to take a seat in a throne, to share His authority.

The Path to the Throne

That command— *"Sit"*—was more than an invitation; it was a direct confrontation with everything I thought I knew about myself.

Up until this point, I had been on a journey of discovering who I was in God's eyes, fighting to understand my identity, to embrace being His son. And now that journey had brought me to a new threshold, one that demanded even more. God wasn't simply asking me to accept being His child; He was inviting me to take up a position as a ruler in His Kingdom. It was one thing to see myself as His servant; that was a position I could understand, even embrace. But to see myself as a ruler seated on a heavenly throne? That felt almost impossible to accept.

The Throne We Forget

It's easy to picture God seated on His throne, high and lifted up, surrounded by heavenly hosts who worship in awe. That image comforts us. And it certainly is the truth of who He is. But As He is so are we in this life. What happens when that image shifts, when suddenly we are asked to position ourselves in a heavenly place of government, sharing in His authority, ruling with Him? For most of us, that feels strange, almost blasphemous. We're quick to kneel as servants, heads bowed low. But to sit and rule alongside Him? To be entrusted with that kind of power and responsibility? For most of us is a lot harder than bowing before him.

Yet, this is exactly what God calls us into. He doesn't just want us as spectators in His Kingdom; He wants us as partners. God isn't only asking for our reverence; He is calling us to rise and rule with Him. He wants us to step into the fullness of His power, to exercise it alongside Him, letting Heaven's life flow through us.

The Battle Within

One of the false voices I was facing was telling me that taking my throne would be prideful. But the opposite is true. Humility is agreeing with who God says we are and accepting the position He has assigned to us. Pride disagrees with God and refuses the position.

I could feel my heart race, doubt still lingering, but I took a deep breath and moved toward the throne, finally allowing myself to sit. I made the choice to be obedient. God had prepared this place for me. To refuse it would have been to deny His design, to reject the very authority He had bestowed upon me.

The Throne Unleashes Life

The instant I touched the seat, a radiant light burst from beneath me, lighting up the darkened landscape around me. The frozen river below me shuddered, cracks spreading through the ice as if it were waking from a long, deep sleep.

Then, the ice shattered, the river rushed down the mountain, flowing into the barren lands below.

As the river flowed, everything it touched transformed. Deserts burst into gardens, trees sprang up, birds sang, the earth itself seemed to breathe again. The sky shed its gray shroud, and golden sunlight poured over the land.

I realised that my absence from this throne had held back life. By refusing to accept my place, I had unknowingly restricted God's power and provision from flowing through me, from reaching the territory within creation that was assigned to me. Creation had been waiting. The authority I was stepping into wasn't about my position; it was about being a a channel for His life. The moment I took my place it activated the flow of heaven through my throne and into creation.

Forgotten Thrones, Waiting Kings

At first, I felt like an imposter, a stranger in a seat that felt too vast, too holy. But God was showing me that this was exactly where He wanted me, exactly where He had planned for me to be.

In His wisdom, God has set up a structure that invites

others to govern alongside Him, and it's not an invitation we can take lightly. He is after all the King of Kings. To refuse this role isn't humility; it's defiance. When we take our place, it doesn't challenge His authority; it completes it. By refusing, we shut down His purpose, closing off part of the life He wants to pour through us.

The truth is, you have a throne. And it's not just a distant promise for eternity; it's a reality that begins right now. Scripture tells us we are seated with Christ in heavenly places. This is not a metaphor; it's a divine truth. The question is, do you believe it? And if you do, will you accept this privilege, this responsibility?

The Power of Your Throne

Your throne is the bridge where Heaven touches Earth. From your throne, you carry and administrate His authority into every area of life. This is where you shift atmospheres, release Heaven's will, and bring transformation to those around you. Sitting in this place, you can channel life into dead places, speak light into darkness, and release the flow of heaven into every situation. This isn't a role to be taken lightly; it's a sacred privilege, a divine calling to let Heaven flow through you.

The Battle for Your Throne

But just like the battle to access heaven, and the battle to step into your identity, there is a battle for your throne. The enemy knows that once you occupy your rightful throne, his influence breaks. When you claim your place, you access a new level of authority that he fears because it obliterates his territory.

That's why the opposition is fierce. The enemy tries to persuade you to avoid your throne saying, *"You're unworthy. You don't belong here."* He clouds your vision, making your destiny seem distant, unreachable. But his lies are only as powerful as we allow them to be. God's invitation is more powerful but must be accepted. It's an invitation to rise, to take your place, and to let Heaven's life flow through you.

The Call to Reign

Will you take the throne prepared for you, or will you remain on the sidelines, living as if you're merely a servant, forgetting that you are a son or daughter of the King? God won't force you, but His invitation is clear. The authority is yours, but it is up to you to sit. Its up to you to accept it.

Chapter 10
Embracing the Divine Call to Responsibility

Psalms 8:6 "You made him ruler over the works of Your hands; You have put all things under his feet."

One day as I was pondering the state of creation and questioning God, asking Him - Father why is creation still in such a mess? I felt God draw me beyond the veil to show me what happened. What he showed me was a beautiful heart that was connected to many organs, but superimposed over this was a heart that was linked to all the planets within the universe. Not a literal connection but an energetic connection. Each beat sending waves of warmth and light across the expanse nourishing creation. This heartbeat that sustained everything around it.

But then, that heartbeat faltered and suddenly, it stopped. The heart got poisoned, and darkness seeped into everything that the heart was supposed to sustain. Streams froze, flowers withered, trees grew brittle and gray, and life itself seemed to withdraw as if creation had taken its last, desperate breath. Silence swept over creation.

God shared with me from a place of deep sadness. *"This is what happened at the fall. Adam was the heartbeat of creation. I entrusted him with dominion. But when he fell, creation fell with him."*

Adam's choice—our choice—opened us up to a poison that infiltrated the rest of creation due to Adams position of dominion and governance. Death entered him and as a direct consequence entered that which he had authority over - all of creation. When darkness entered, creation itself went into mourning, waiting for the day that it once again come into the glorious liberty of the Sons. And with that realization, I was overcome with a weight of responsibility. We caused the downfall of creation. We were entrusted with the sacred responsibility of dominion and our actions lead to the fall of creation.

From Awakening to Purpose

The ache of this responsibility pressed upon me, and I understood: that as we accept our access to heaven, as we accept our identity as we accept our position, with that position comes a great responsibility. The responsibility and authority to govern creation. My choices, my authority, my acceptance of my position has repercussions beyond my own life. Just like Adams decision had repercussions beyond his own life. This wasn't just about my redemption; it was about the redemption of all creation that would take place as a domino effect.

The same way that Adam's fall caused a cosmic collapse, our redemption causes a cosmic resurgence—a continuous ripple of light that emanates from our throne that restores creation itself, healing every wound and realigning every atom, every star. By accepting our position we reclaim every realm affected by the fall. This goes beyond the earth. The bible doesn't say the earth is groaning waiting for redemption, it says all of creation. Therefore all of creation is intrinsically connected to the condition of the Sons. Think about a stone dropped into a still lake, ripples flowing out from a center point. This is what it looks like in the realm of the spirit when you occupy your throne, waves of light flow out awakening creation to come back into alignment with its original state.

Creation's Groan for Redemption

Creation is calling out, "Where are you, guardians? Will you rise?" It's not waiting for God to intervene directly but looking to us—the Sons of God—for redemption. Scripture doesn't say creation is groaning for God; rather, it groans for us. Why? God is our salvation, yet we are the salvation of creation. He has entrusted us with the responsibility to govern, to have dominion over the works of His hands.

Creation is instinctively turning to us for healing. Once, we brought darkness, but now we hold the power to bring light. Every river, forest, and creature is intrinsically connected to us, mirroring our condition, waiting for us to reclaim our rightful role and to breathe Heaven back into Earth.

Radah: The Ancient Mandate

From the beginning, God gave us a mandate, a divine responsibility to govern with love. To establish Heaven's order on Earth. In Hebrew, the word *radah* (רָדָה) means to rule, to take responsibility—not as harsh masters, but as loving caretakers. This isn't a suggestion; it's a commandment etched into the core of our being.

Imagine the scene again—the shock wave that tore through creation when Adam fell, the silence that swept over life. Now, imagine the opposite: sons and daughters, fully awakened, returning to their roles, reclaiming their authority in Christ. Imagine deserts blooming, clean rivers flowing, creation flourishing. When we step into our mandate, creation responds.

This is what *radah* means. It is a delegated authority from the Sovereign God of the universe to oversee the works of his hands and to ensure the wellbeing of creation. WE are the ones who restore harmony. This is why the Bible says Christ in us is the hope of glory, not Christ in heaven the hope of glory. Because we are the ones that hold the key to the great restoration.

The Throne of Responsibility & The Call to Restoration

When Jesus prayed, "On Earth as it is in Heaven," He was depending on us to collaborate with him to fulfill his desire. Heaven and earth unified, to the point where you cannot distinguish the two from one another. A merging of the dimensions.

The Lion King

illustrates this truth so beautifully. Simba allowed his

kingdom to come under the dominion of darkness by running away from his throne. Only by coming into agreement with His father, the truth about his identity, position and responsibility to rule, did the land flourish once again. It responded to a king who took his place. When he roared from his throne, creation responded, light returned and the land flourished once again. Creation is watching, as Sons are now stepping up and taking their place.

Heaven on Earth

Our calling isn't about escaping to Heaven someday; it's about administrating the government of Heaven into the environment around us here and now. We weren't designed to abandon Earth but to stand as bridges, as gates between the dimensions letting Heaven flow through us. Each of us holds the power to bring transformation, to answer creation's call by stepping into the responsibility that was always ours.

This should wake us up. It should shake us. We're not insignificant; we are rulers, heirs of the Kingdom. Carriers of divine authority. Our choices shape creation, our words carry the power of life, and our presence can restore a broken world.

Chapter 11
The Throne Awaits

This is your crossing point, this is your moment.

The same moment that Simba faced, when he encountered his father.

Your moment to step in and step up.

Step through the veil with me and see - before you stands a throne—ancient, eternal, it is carved with your name. It is not just a seat; it is your place of authority and divine purpose set aside for you since the beginning of time. This throne, your throne, carries a weight no one else can bear, because it was made for you alone.

This throne has waited patiently, knowing that only you could fill this place. It doesn't care about your accomplishments or titles, but it recognises the essence of who you are.

The Father is standing there asking you a question.

Will you sit?

Will you accept the position I have made for you in my Kingdom?

If you hesitate, know that there is no shame.

The gravity of this throne holds the full weight of Heaven itself. But the invitation is clear. Sitting here means stepping fully into the life you were created to lead, becoming the conduit through which Heaven's life flows into the world. It means embracing the role that God has assigned to you.

So, will you sit? Will you accept the invitation?

The Power of the Throne

As you lower yourself onto the throne, a surge of power envelops you.

Your throne begins to pulse with life, energy, and purpose, activating a strength that reaches beyond your own.

Heaven's begins to pulse through you reminding you of the authority you carry and the divine partnership you have been called to embrace.

You are here, as a king to serve creation. From this place, God's justice, love, and wisdom are ready to flow through you, reaching into all the corners of creation. Feel the weight of this calling, the warmth of Heaven's presence, as you take your rightful place.

As you sit, you remember who you are, you remember your divine origin, you remember your divine mandate, you look into creation as an authorized and appointed governor. One who has been given dominion.

The Vision Unleashed

As you sit, a river beneath your throne starts flowing healing and restoring everything that it touches.

Can you see it? The ripple outward, coming from your throne, touching places and people beyond your imagination.

This is your mandate. This is your legacy. As a son, as an heir, as a king. You begin to witness a world transformed by Heaven's touch through you.

Creation itself now recognizes the authority you carry, bending, aligning, and blooming as you claim this place.

The Weight of Acceptance

This throne has always been yours, carrying the knowledge of your blueprint, the knowledge of your destiny.

Its time to accept this responsibility fully and own the power that has been entrusted to you.

This throne was always here, ready, prepared, waiting.

AS you choose to embrace your authority and take dominion, know that this is your permanent place of positioning. You are now positioned here. You notice that all of heaven has turned towards you cheering and acknowledging you as you take your rightful place

Epilogue: The Return to the Throne

I close my eyes, and suddenly, I'm eight years old again. My face is pressed against the airplane window, watching the only home I knew slip away beneath the clouds. I can still see that little boy—his heart wide open, his spirit wild and free, a smile of wonder on his face. He was filled with joyful anticipation of what would wait for him on the other side. Little did he know that his world would turn dark for more than 10 years. That boy had no idea of the darkness he would face. If I could reach through time, I would sit beside him, hold his little hand, and whisper, "You're about to face pain you can't yet imagine. There will be days when nothing makes sense, and you'll wonder why this is happening to you. But none of it is your fault. You'll feel lost, abandoned, and betrayed, but remember: God has a plan."

There's so much I would say to that boy. I'd tell him that when he reaches the end of himself, when the world seems to turn its back, God will keep His promise. He will find him; He will save him. I'd tell him the journey won't be easy, but he'll gain infinitely more than he ever lost.

As I look back at the boy who once watched Africa disappear below him, I see now that he wasn't losing his home—he was being prepared for a greater one. And as I look forward, I know the journey isn't over. Each step I take opens the way for countless others to step into their own calling, to claim their own throne.

I would tell my parents that they made the right choice. A choice that came with immeasurable sacrifice, but I would thank them for having the courage to follow the call of God on our lives.

The Power of Redemption

And here I am, looking back from the other side of that

journey. Life has come full circle, and every broken piece has been redeemed in ways I could never have imagined. That beautiful woman I met in Jeffrey's Bay, Jazz—my best friend, I am now honored to call my wife. She has been my source of wisdom and strength for 14 years, grounding me when I lost direction, inspiring me when I doubted myself. Sacrificing her own wishes for the greater good. I couldn't be more grateful for her presence, her support and belief in me a gift I never take for granted.

Together, we've shared a lifetime's worth of adventures, each one carving its place in our story. Like swimming out to w whale together (very dangerous). And driving halfway up Africa, from South Africa to Kenya, across wild terrain. Along the way, we encountered both beauty and danger, including being hijacked by Somalian pirates who stole all our money—a tale perhaps for another day. I can still remember the thrill of crossing into Burma, exploring Thailand, traveling thorough Namibia. We spent 6 years living in rural Australia which for Jazz was a massive sacrifice. We lived in Toronto Canada for a year and a half which was an incredible experience. We've lived in New Zealand, each new place leaving its mark on us, expanding our vision of the world and our role within it.

Our journeys weren't only about the places; they were about the people. We've been privileged to be part of vibrant communities across continents, working and serving alongside incredible souls from all walks of life. From village projects in South Africa to faith communities in the States, we've found family in strangers and learned lessons that bridged cultures and beliefs. Each community became a chapter in our story, each person a reminder of the power of connection and shared purpose.

And then came the greatest gifts of all—our children, Blaze and Zariya. They are the embodiment of our love, the living proof of redemption and possibility, and they bring us a joy that words can barely contain. Blaze, with his boundless curiosity and zest for life, and Zariya, with her gentle spirit and fierce creativity, have taught us more about love and resilience than any journey ever could. They remind me daily of the incredible redemption that has taken place in my life, of promises fulfilled, of dreams surpassed.

In these moments of reflection, I see that everything—the roads we traveled, the risks we took, the love we built—is part of a tapestry woven by a greater hand, each thread a story of redemption and purpose. And as I look forward, I know the journey isn't over. We're still moving, still learning, still stepping into the calling that brought us together. Together, as a family, we are living proof that life, even in its wildest storms, can be redeemed, restored, and used for something far beyond what we could ever imagine. I've been blessed with mentors from around the globe who have deeply invested in my spiritual, relational, and financial life.

The boy who didn't make it through school went on to earn a master's degree in business—not because of academic talent, but through divine guidance and favor.

My relationship with my parents is better than ever; they are truly the best parents I could have asked for. God has been faithful in bringing our whole family along in the path of redemption and I have so much honour and respect for my parents.

New Zealand has become a place of blessing that I cherish deeply. It is a country where I've found incredible friends. It has enriched and refined me, but it has also gifted me with experiences that have shaped who I am. It has given me wealth and opened up the world to me and my family. I love New Zealand and hold it close to my heart. Even though I went through years of pain here, I wouldn't change anything about the past and the difficulties I had to face.

Through this journey, I've built a life overflowing with abundance from a realm beyond this world. God's favor has been extraordinary. One day, I may write another book on our journey in business, investment, and wealth. Today, I oversee an investment portfolio, a thriving coaching and training business, an online community that empowers people to unlock their purpose, and I'm actively involved in a global foundation with a mission to impact the world. Through my online training community, Infinite Academy I'm privileged to help others step into their own divine calling, freeing themselves from lives that once felt trapped.

I am here to use everything I've learned—every scar and every blessing—to help others step into their divine place. My mission is to awaken as many sons and daughters as possible, to guide them toward the same truth that changed my life: that they, too, are called to sit on a throne, to reign with purpose, and to bring Heaven's grace to Earth.

If there's one truth I want to leave with you, it's this: each of us has a throne waiting, a place in God's Kingdom that no one else can fill. That throne isn't about status; it's about the unique purpose placed on your life. This is your invitation—just as it was mine—to rise above the labels, limitations, and lies that have tried to hold you back. You weren't created to remain small; you were born to rise.

This is my prayer, my hope, and my purpose—that you, too, will rise. That you will take your place in the Kingdom and live out of the fullness of who you were created to be.

I bless you and I bless your journey with all the love in my heart.

An Invitation to Rise

I would love to connect with you and want to personally invite you to join my online community where we have live calls, resources and training to step into the fullness of what God has for us. For more resources, or to join my online community and meet others who are being empowered along this journey, please visit www.robbieventer.com

Thank You

To everyone who has walked alongside me on this journey, my deepest gratitude. Thank you for your love, kindness, and support. Thank you for walking in the Spirit, for believing in me, and for being an unwavering source of inspiration. Your faithfulness to the call on your life has been a powerful encouragement to me, and I am profoundly grateful for each of you.

I cannot possibly acknowledge all my friends here as the list would be too long, but I want to thank the mentors and leaders who inspired me in this journey.

To Jazz, Blaze, and Zariya—my beloved wife and children. You are my heart and my joy. Jazz, your strength, wisdom, and love are my foundation, and Blaze and Zariya, your light and laughter remind me daily of life's greatest gifts.

To my Mother and Father —thank you for your love and sacrifices, for your prayer and for instilling in me the values and faith that guide me.

To Hannro—love you, bro. Thank you for always being there.

To Cobus and Henda - Thank you for the way you raised your daughter and for always being there for us

To my Ouma and Tannie Dolfie—thank you for your prayers and for making that phone call. Your wisdom and kindness has changed my life.

Tannie Sanet – Thank you for your love and support

Tannie Magda and Oom Peet – Thanks for taking me to the Lion King and your amazing hospitality

To Des and Cara Sawyer—thank you for your accepting me when it really counted

Ian and Kay Clayton - Thank you for loving me through my brokeness

Barry and Angie Ward - Thank you for giving me an opportunity at such a young age, love you guys

Marios and Danielle Ellinas - We knew we were going to journey together forever from the day we met, love you guys

Lindi Masters - Thank you for believing in me and opening up a platform for me, I am really grateful for your faith in me

Dale and Karen - Your love and generosity inspires me, thank you for inviting us to be with you and for helping me to think bigger

To the Ariel team - Thank you to everyone in Ariel who inspire me every day with your dedication, generosity and courage.

Tricia McDonald - You are such an inspiration to me Tricia - thank you for believing in and empowering the next generation.

Infinite Academy - The infinite group you guys will change the world.

Graeme and Dianne - For thinking big, taking risks and being obedient to the call

Warren and Annette - Thank you for loving us so well

Grant and Sam Mahoney - Your investment into us and into the Nest community was life changing for me - thank you

Andy and Janine Mason - Your dedication to empower people is incredible, thank you

The Nexus team - Josh, Jodz, Jared, Reanna - love you guys

Bay City Outreach Centre - Thank you to the team at Bay City for your input into my family

Victory Christian Church - Thank you to Victory Christian Church for setting up the VGY program

Professionally - I have had a lot of help with this book - Thank you to Leilani Hayes, Elbie Swanepoel, Joanna Barton, Liz Beasse, Jacob Morey. You guys have been incredible in your willingness to help me get my ideas on paper. Thank you for your hard work and dedication in bringing this project to life.

Friends - To all my friends who are too many to name here (you know who you are). I love you and I am grateful to you.

And to you, the reader—thank you for paying the price to embark on this journey with me. Your presence here is a testament to your own courage and readiness to step into your purpose. May this book be a blessing to you.

With all my gratitude,
Robbie

Made in United States
Orlando, FL
18 July 2025